anythink

U0567944

TIBET

Joseph Harris

Marshall Cavendish
Benchmark
New York

This edition first published in 2010 in the United States of America by
MARSHALL CAVENDISH BENCHMARK
An imprint of Marshall Cavendish Corporation

All rights reserved.

No part of this publication may be reproduced, stored in a retrieval system or transmitted, in any form or by
any means, electronic, mechanical, photocopying, recording, or otherwise, without the prior permission of the
copyright owner. Request for permission should be addressed to the Publisher, Marshall Cavendish Corporation,
99 White Plains Road, Tarrytown, NY 10591. Tel: (914) 332-8888, fax: (914) 332-1888.

Website: www.marshallcavendish.us

This publication represents the opinions and views of the author based on Joseph Harris's personal experience,
knowledge, and research. The information in this book serves as a general guide only. The author and publisher
have used their best efforts in preparing this book and disclaim liability rising directly and indirectly from the
use and application of this book.

Other Marshall Cavendish Offices:
Marshall Cavendish Ltd. 5th Floor, 32-38 Saffron Hill, London EC1N 8 FH, UK • Marshall Cavendish International
(Asia) Private Limited, 1 New Industrial Road, Singapore 536196 • Marshall Cavendish International (Thailand)
Co Ltd. 253 Asoke, 12th Flr, Sukhumvit 21 Road, Klongtoey Nua, Wattana, Bangkok 10110, Thailand • Marshall
Cavendish (Malaysia) Sdn Bhd, Times Subang, Lot 46, Subang Hi-Tech Industrial Park, Batu Tiga, 40000 Shah
Alam, Selangor Darul Ehsan, Malaysia

Marshall Cavendish is a trademark of Times Publishing Limited

All websites were available and accurate when this book was sent to press.

Library of Congress Cataloging-in-Publication Data

Harris, Joseph, date
    Tibet / Joseph Harris.
       p. cm. — (Global hotspots)
    Summary: "Discusses Tibet, its history, conflicts, and the reasons why it is currently in the news"—Provided
by publisher.
    Includes index.
    ISBN 978-0-7614-4762-7
    1. Tibet (China)—Juvenile literature. I. Title.
    DS786.H334 2011
951'.5—dc22

                                          2009039776

First published in 2010 by
MACMILLAN EDUCATION AUSTRALIA PTY LTD
15–19 Claremont Street, South Yarra 3141

Visit our website at www.macmillan.com.au or go directly to www.macmillanlibrary.com.au

Associated companies and representatives throughout the world.

Copyright © Macmillan Education Australia 2010

 Produced for Macmillan Education Australia by
MONKEY PUZZLE MEDIA LTD
48 York Avenue, Hove BN3 1PJ, UK

Edited by Susie Brooks
Text and cover design by Tom Morris and James Winrow
Page layout by Tom Morris
Photo research by Susie Brooks and Lynda Lines
Maps by Martin Darlison, Encompass Graphics

Printed in the United States

Acknowledgments
The author and the publisher are grateful to the following for permission to reproduce copyright material:

Front cover photograph: Police arrest a Tibetan nun during a protest by Tibetan exiles in Kathmandu, Nepal.
Courtesy of Reuters (Gopal Chitrakar).

Corbis, **9** (Leonard de Selva), **10** (Hulton-Deutsch Collection), **12** (Bettmann), **13** (Bettmann), **14** (Bettmann),
16 (Bettmann), **17** (Bettmann), **20** (Bettmann), **21** (Bettmann), **22** (Bettmann), **23** (Dean Conger), **24** (Bettmann),
26 (Bettmann), **28** (Reuters); Getty Images, **4** (AFP), **8** (Hulton Archive), **11** (Popperfoto), **15** (Popperfoto), **18** (AFP),
19 (Time & Life Pictures), **25** (Matthieu Ricard), **27**, **29** (AFP); iStockphoto, **30**; MPM Images **6**.

While every care has been taken to trace and acknowledge copyright, the publisher tenders their apologies for any
accidental infringement where copyright has proved untraceable. Where the attempt has been unsuccessful, the
publisher welcomes information that would redress the situation.

1 3 5 6 4 2

CONTENTS

Glossary Words

When a word is printed in **bold**, you can look
up its meaning in the Glossary on page 31.

ALWAYS IN THE NEWS

Global hot spots are places that are always in the news. They are places where there has been conflict between different groups of people for years. Sometimes the conflicts have lasted for hundreds of years.

Why Do Hot Spots Happen?

There are four main reasons why hot spots happen:

1 Disputes over land, and who has the right to live on it.

2 Disagreements over religion and **culture**, where different peoples find it impossible to live happily side-by-side.

3 Arguments over how the government should be organized.

4 Conflict over resources, such as oil, gold, or diamonds.

Sometimes these disagreements spill over into violence—and into the headlines.

HOT SPOT BRIEFING

FORBIDDEN CITY
The capital of Tibet, Lhasa, used to be known as "the Forbidden City." Lhasa was remote and hard to reach. Its religious leaders believed it was a holy city and wanted to keep out strangers who might interfere with Tibetan traditions.

In 2008, a truck holding Chinese riot police passes the Potala Palace in Lhasa. This was the traditional home of Tibet's religious leader, the Dalai Lama.

Tibet as a Hot Spot

Tibet has been a hot spot since 1950, when Chinese forces took over. The Chinese government claims that Tibet is part of China. But many Tibetans strongly oppose Chinese rule and the changes that the Chinese leaders have introduced.

Religion

Most Tibetans are **Buddhists**. Religion has a big influence on Tibetan life. For centuries the chief Buddhist **monk**, the Dalai Lama, was the most powerful person in Tibet. The present Dalai Lama lives in **exile** because of his opposition to the Chinese.

As this map shows, many Tibetans live in parts of China outside the Tibet Autonomous Region. Some Tibetans would like to form a larger, self-governing Tibet that would include these regions.

HOT SPOT BRIEFING

TIBETAN PEOPLE
Tibetans are a distinct people, with their own language and culture. They are one of many **minorities** within China. Many Tibetans live outside the area China calls the Tibet Autonomous Region.

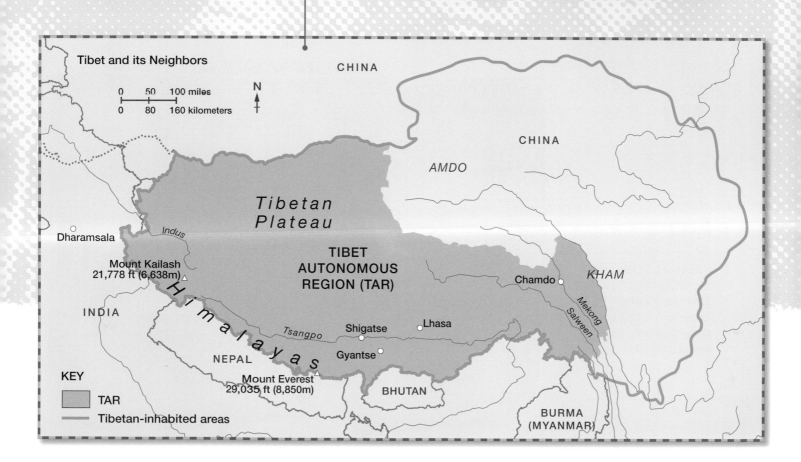

Tibet and its Neighbors

0   50   100 miles
0   80   160 kilometers

N

CHINA

CHINA

AMDO

Tibetan Plateau

Dharamsala

Indus

Mount Kailash
21,778 ft (6,638m)

TIBET
AUTONOMOUS
REGION (TAR)

Chamdo

KHAM

Himalayas

INDIA

Tsangpo

Shigatse

Lhasa

Mekong
Salween

Gyantse

NEPAL

Mount Everest
29,035 ft (8,850m)

KEY

TAR

Tibetan-inhabited areas

BHUTAN

BURMA
(MYANMAR)

A BUDDHIST KINGDOM

Early in its history, Tibet was a powerful kingdom. In some later periods, the Chinese **Empire** controlled Tibet. This is why China claims that Tibet is not an independent country but a part of China.

Royalty and Religion

In the 600s and 700s CE, warlike kings ruled Tibet. In about 641 CE, a Tibetan king was converted to Buddhism, which soon became Tibet's main religion. During the 800s, the Tibetan **monarchy** collapsed and the kingdom was divided between rival nobles.

HOT SPOT BRIEFING

REINCARNATION
Buddhism teaches that when a living being dies, it is reborn into a new body. This is called reincarnation.

Statues in a Tibetan temple honor King Songtsen Gampo and two of his wives. The king is said to have been responsible for bringing Buddhism to Tibet.

Tibet and the Chinese Empire

In the 1240s, China conquered Tibet. The Chinese emperor appointed a Tibetan religious leader, or *lama*, to rule the land. The Tibetans saw the Chinese emperor as their **overlord**. But by the 1400s, political changes in China had greatly weakened Chinese influence over Tibet.

The Dalai Lamas

During the 1600s, Tibet's religious leader began to be known as the Dalai (or "oceanwide") Lama. Each Dalai Lama remained leader until his death. At times when Chinese control was weak, the Dalai Lama was Tibet's political ruler, as well as being its religious leader.

HOT SPOT BRIEFING

THE CHINESE CLAIM
China's claim to have ruled Tibet from the 1200s is important today. Modern Chinese governments argue that it proves that Tibet is part of China. People who favor Tibetan independence reject the argument.

The Mongols were an Asian people who created a huge empire, shown here at the height of its power. The Mongol emperor of China also controlled Tibet, and modern Chinese claims that Tibet is part of China are partly based on this fact.

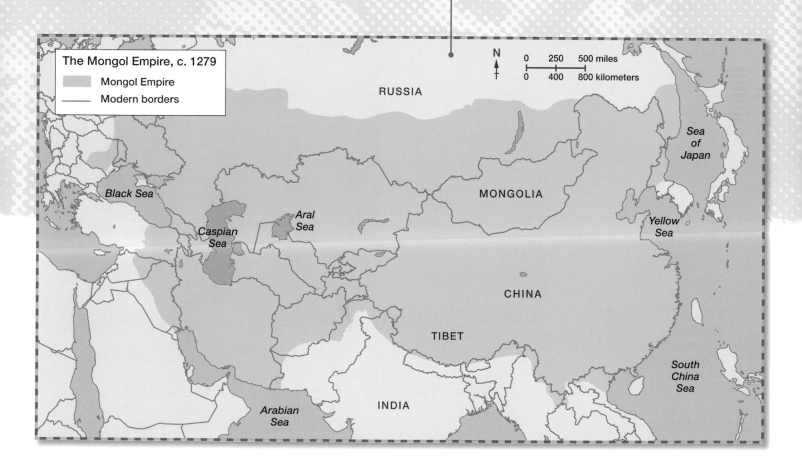

The Mongol Empire, c. 1279
- Mongol Empire
- Modern borders

N

| 0 | 250 | 500 miles |
| 0 | 400 | 800 kilometers |

RUSSIA

Sea of Japan

Black Sea

Aral Sea

Caspian Sea

MONGOLIA

Yellow Sea

CHINA

TIBET

South China Sea

Arabian Sea

INDIA

TIBET AND THE GREAT POWERS

In the 1900s, the rival empires of Britain and Russia turned their attention toward Tibet. Neither side wanted the other to gain control over the region.

British Expedition

Tibet shared a border with British-ruled India. Britain feared that Russia could gain power in the region by invading Tibet. In 1903–1904, a British military force fought its way into Tibet to make sure that Tibet would not act against Britain's interests. When the British reached the capital, Lhasa, the Tibetans were forced to make an agreement with them.

"There entered the peaceful valley all the horrors of war—dead and maimed men in the streets and houses, burning villages, death and destruction of all kinds."

Daily Mail newspaper correspondent Edmund Candler, who traveled with the British expedition, describes the suffering it caused.

In this painting, a representative from Colonel Younghusband's 1903–1904 British expedition meets with Tibetans. The Tibetans put up a brave but hopeless resistance to the British advance.

Chinese Fears

Britain's and Russia's interest in Tibet stirred up fears in China. Although the Chinese had a representative in Lhasa, called an *Amban*, they did not normally interfere much in Tibetan life. But the prospect of foreign powers moving into Tibet made the Chinese want to control it more directly.

A Brief Invasion

In 1910, China sent an army to take control of Tibet. The Chinese Empire had decided that it was time to claim the land it had conquered nearly 700 years before. But in 1911 the Chinese Empire collapsed, and in 1912 China became a **republic**. With China in turmoil, the Tibetans seized the chance to drive out Chinese troops.

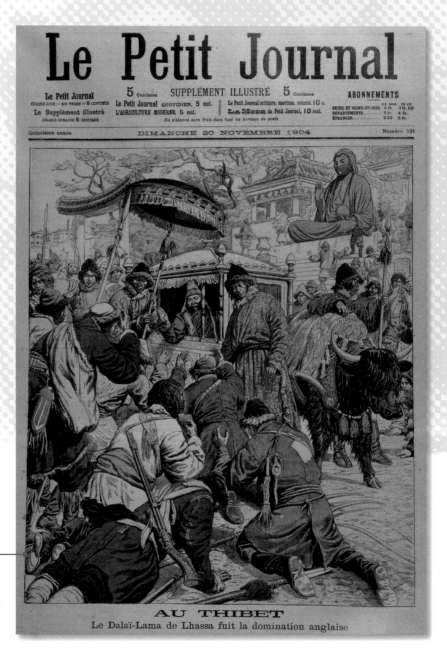

HOT SPOT BRIEFING

TREATIES
In 1904, the British and Tibetans signed a **treaty**. This treaty implied that Britain recognized Tibet as an independent country. But in 1907, Britain and Russia changed their policies and agreed to recognize Tibet as a part of China.

A French newspaper from 1904 reports on the British expedition to Tibet: "The Dalai Lama flees from English domination." Lower ranking officials were left to make a treaty with the British.

INDEPENDENT TIBET: 1912–1950

From 1912 until 1950, Tibet governed itself. Chinese leaders still regarded Tibet as part of China, but wars and **civil wars** prevented them from enforcing their claim. Meanwhile, life in Tibet went on much as it had for centuries.

A Traditional Society

Tibet was a highly traditional society. Buddhism played an important role in everyday life. Ordinary Tibetans took part enthusiastically in religious festivals. Many Tibetans became monks or nuns. Monks alone made up about 10 percent of the population!

Religion and Inequality

Tibet was a very unequal society with a rigid caste system. Its people were born into a fixed caste, or rank, which they could not change. In the early 1900s, some Tibetans were still slaves.

A group of child monks gather to be photographed in 1938. Boys were sent away from their families to become monks while they were still very young.

Ruling Classes

The Dalai Lama ruled with the help of a group of noble advisers called the *Kashag*. When a Dalai Lama died, a young child was chosen to follow him, so nobles ruled on his behalf until he grew up.

Crime and Punishment

In traditional Tibet, criminals were brutally treated. Some crimes were punished by cutting off hands or feet, or gouging out eyes. Severe beatings and whippings were common. However, some Tibetans claim that conditions began to improve in the 1900s.

"We cannot revert [go back] to the old Tibet, and even if we could, we do not want to, because there were many things wrong with our society."

Tenzin Gyatso, the fourteenth Dalai Lama, speaking to the British newspaper, the *Independent,* in 2004.

In 1938, when this photograph was taken, the four-year-old Tenzin Gyatso had already been recognized as the reincarnation and successor of the thirteenth Dalai Lama, who had died in 1933.

CHINA TAKES OVER

In 1950, China invaded Tibet. The Chinese quickly defeated the Tibetans and took control. They claimed to be freeing the Tibetan people, but few Tibetans welcomed their arrival.

Appeal for Help

The Tibetan authorities appealed to the **United Nations** (UN) for help. But it was unclear whether the UN had the right to interfere. Was Tibet an independent country that had been invaded, or a historic part of China? In the end, the UN did not act.

The Chinese army moves into Tibet in 1950, building a bridge across a river and bringing over a motor vehicle on a raft. The Tibetans stood little chance against the Chinese and their modern equipment.

HOT SPOT BRIEFING

COMMUNISM
In 1949, a communist government took power in China. Communist beliefs are very different from traditional Tibetan ones. Communists believed:
- land should not be owned by individuals, but shared
- everyone should be equal
- religion had no place in society.

Seventeen Point Agreement

The Tibetans realized that they could not stand up to the Chinese People's Liberation Army (PLA). Instead, they agreed to a treaty called the "Seventeen Point Agreement." By signing the document, the Tibetans accepted that Tibet was part of China. In return, the Chinese promised that they would not introduce extreme **reforms** in Tibet. Tibetan traditions would be respected. The Chinese agreed to let the Dalai Lama remain the head of his people.

HOT SPOT BRIEFING

BEYOND TIBET
Beyond the official borders of Tibet lay regions called Kham and Amdo. The people who lived there were Tibetans. But China included most of Kham and Amdo in its western **provinces**, and did not consider them part of Tibet.

Chinese leader Mao Zedong (center) meets the Dalai Lama (right) and Tibet's second most important monk, the Panchen Lama (left), in 1956. During this period, the Tibetan leaders did not openly oppose Chinese rule.

REBELLION AGAINST CHINA

In 1956, the Tibetans living in the regions of Kham and Amdo revolted against Chinese rule. Because they were not living in Tibet, they had not been protected from communist reforms by the Seventeen Point Agreement.

The Tibetans who first resisted the Chinese were nomads like these women. Having always owned their own animals and traveled the land freely, they hated communist reforms.

Rebel Anger

The rebels were angry because the communists were trying to change their way of life. The Chinese forced **nomads**, who roamed the land with their animals, to settle and become farmers. Those who were already farmers had their lands taken away to be shared equally by everyone.

HOT SPOT BRIEFING

CIA SUPPORT
The United States of America opposed communism, so its **Central Intelligence Agency (CIA)** secretly supported the Tibetan rebels. It helped to train **guerrilla** fighters, and supplied them with weapons.

Unrest Spreads

The unrest spread as many rebels fled into Tibet. News of what the communists had done in Kham and Amdo led to fears about what they would eventually do in Tibet itself.

Lhasa Uprising

In 1959, fears that the Chinese planned to kidnap the Dalai Lama led to unrest in the Tibetan capital, Lhasa. Tibetan demonstrations were stopped by Chinese PLA troops. While Tibetans clashed with the PLA, the Dalai Lama fled into exile in northern India. Tibetan guerrilla fighters continued to battle against Chinese forces until 1962. In the end the PLA defeated the rebellion.

STATISTICS

TIBETAN CASUALTIES

Tibetan nationalist sources claim that 86,000 Tibetans were killed during the Lhasa uprising. China denies this and claims that the rebels did not have widespread support.

The Dalai Lama (center, on a white pony) flees to India following the Lhasa uprising of 1959. In exile, he went on to campaign for greater freedom in Tibet.

AFTER THE REBELLION

After the Lhasa uprising, the Chinese changed their policy in Tibet. They accused the Dalai Lama and the Tibetan nobles of plotting the revolt. China said that the Seventeen Point Agreement had been broken.

Change Begins

The Chinese began to bring in changes to make Tibet more like the rest of communist China. The communists had always wanted to create a more equal society, but had been prevented from making changes in Tibet by the Seventeen Point Agreement.

HOT SPOT BRIEFING

REFORMS IN TIBET
To make Tibet into a communist society, the Chinese government introduced reforms, including:
- taking land from the rich and giving it to the poor
- stopping peasants from having to work for landlords
- reducing rents.

In 1964, Tibetan schoolchildren play tug of war. The Chinese set up new schools and gave Tibetan children wider educational opportunities.

Nobles

For centuries, Tibetan nobles and monks had lived off earnings from the lands they owned. Land reform took away much of their wealth. Many nobles were given paid official positions and could go on with their traditional way of life. But those who had supported the revolt were punished.

Mixed Feelings About Change

Ordinary Tibetans had mixed feelings about Chinese policies. Many people were pleased to be given land of their own. But they still viewed the Chinese as interfering outsiders.

"We ... who were the most unfortunate in Tibet, were happy. But ... we hoped that [the Chinese] would not stay too long."

A poor Tibetan peasant's response to the communist land reforms.

Poor peasants benefited from communist land reforms. In the old Tibet they had worked the lands of nobles and wealthier peasants for little pay.

TIBETANS IN EXILE

Many Tibetans fled from their Chinese-dominated land and became exiles. The largest exile community formed at Dharamsala in neighboring India, where the Dalai Lama lived after 1959.

The Dalai Lama speaks to the press in 2008, after nearly fifty years in exile. With international attention focused on recent riots in Lhasa, he put forward serious criticisms of China's policies.

Government in Exile

Tibetan exiles in India set up an alternative government of Tibet, called a government in exile, headed by the Dalai Lama. In 1960, they formed an elected **parliament**, which still exists. Its members represent the various exile communities, and the traditional Tibetan regions and Buddhist **sects**.

HOT SPOT BRIEFING

DALAI LAMA
The fourteenth Dalai Lama, Tenzin Gyatso, was born in 1935. Since his exile in 1959, he has always condemned violence and supported only peaceful protest. He was awarded the Nobel Peace Prize in 1989. In December 2008, he announced his retirement from his active leadership role.

International Campaign

The Dalai Lama and the Tibetan exile community began an international campaign, telling the world about their country's problems. They generated a great deal of sympathy for Tibet's situation, especially among people in **Western** nations.

International Action

Governments around the world took little action over Tibet. This was because Tibet is widely recognized as being a part of China. Countries do not normally interfere in one another's home affairs.

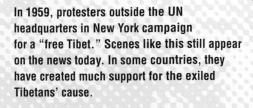

HOT SPOT BRIEFING

UN RESOLUTIONS
In 1959, 1961 and 1965, the UN General Assembly passed **resolutions** criticizing China's **human rights** record in Tibet. However, no similar resolution has been adopted since the communist government of China was allowed to join the UN in 1971.

In 1959, protesters outside the UN headquarters in New York campaign for a "free Tibet." Scenes like this still appear on the news today. In some countries, they have created much support for the exiled Tibetans' cause.

TIBET AUTONOMOUS REGION

In 1965, China established the Tibet Autonomous Region (TAR). China did this to make Tibet more fully part of China. Although autonomous means "self-governing," Tibet had only limited power to decide its own affairs.

A New Form of Rule

Tibet was now to be ruled as a normal part of China. The power of the local nobles was to be weakened. A Tibetan branch of the Chinese Communist Party was set up, and a new governing body, called the People's Congress, was formed.

HOT SPOT BRIEFING

ELECTIONS
The Communist Party held elections to choose members for Tibet's first People's Congress. However, there was no real choice, since only pro-communists were allowed to stand for election.

In 1965, Tibetans cast their votes for the first Tibetan People's Congress of the Tibet Autonomous Region. In reality, Tibetans had very limited powers of self-government.

Convincing the Tibetans

The Chinese government tried to convince ordinary Tibetans that communism was better than the old ways. The Chinese taught the peasants communist theory and recruited them into the Party.

Struggle Sessions

At special meetings, called "struggle sessions," the peasants were encouraged to tell how badly they had been treated by landowners. Many nobles were condemned, even if they had previously sided with the Chinese. They were deliberately humiliated, and some were imprisoned or **executed**.

HOT SPOT BRIEFING

COMMUNES

Tibetans were forced to join special group-run farms called communes. This was supposed to be the next step toward an ideal communist society. In communes, everything was shared equally by the group. Tibetan peasants disliked the new system. They were reluctant to hand back the land that the communists had so recently given to them.

This government publicity picture shows a former beggar, now said to be a happy and prosperous worker. Images like this often contained some truth, but rarely the whole truth.

THE CULTURAL REVOLUTION

In 1966, the Chinese Communist Party launched the "Cultural Revolution," a campaign to replace traditional ideas all over China with communist values. In Tibet, this meant an all-out attack on Buddhism.

Red Guards

In China, young communist extremists formed units called Red Guards. Their aim was to destroy the old culture and uncover enemies of communism. The Cultural Revolution caused chaos in Tibet and throughout China.

"The Red Guards cut off my hair… They cut off one plait [braid], but left the other one so that I could be pulled on and off the stage during struggle sessions."

A Tibetan woman describes her harsh treatment during the Cultural Revolution.

These very young Red Guards carry a large portrait of Chairman Mao. Red Guards, often students, attacked everyone and everything they saw as opposing communist ideas.

Attack on Tradition

The Red Guards forced Tibetans to give up traditional ceremonies. They destroyed many buildings and precious objects. Tibet's monasteries were obvious targets. The Guards were anti-religious, and thought the monks had mistreated the peasants. The Red Guards did so much damage that the Tibetan countryside is still covered with ruined monasteries.

1969 Revolt

In 1969, a Buddhist revolt broke out. It was led by a nun, Thrinley Choedron. She and her supporters launched savage attacks, killing and wounding Chinese. Eventually they were defeated by the PLA and Choedron was executed.

HOT SPOT BRIEFING

TIBETAN REDS
Some young Tibetans were convinced by communist **propaganda** and became Red Guards. They helped to destroy Tibet's monasteries. Some later said that they regretted their actions.

Tibetan monks gather in the remains of Gandan monastery, near Lhasa. This great monastery suffered severe damage during the Cultural Revolution.

RESTORATION OF ORDER

By 1970, it was clear that the campaign of destruction by the Red Guards had gone too far. The PLA stepped in to restore order. But much of Tibet's **heritage** had already been destroyed.

New Landscape

The Cultural Revolution had transformed the Tibetan landscape. Portraits of the Dalai Lama had been torn down and replaced with pictures of the Chinese leader, Chairman Mao. The monasteries lay in ruins. Traditional Tibetan clothing had been replaced with plain Chinese uniforms.

HOT SPOT BRIEFING

COMMUNIST INFIGHTING
During the Cultural Revolution, the communists in Tibet had split into two rival groups who fought each other. In 1970, the PLA moved in and stopped the fighting. The leaders of both groups were condemned.

A portrait of Chairman Mao Zedong hangs in place of the Buddha in Lhasa's Ramoqe Temple. During the Cultural Revolution, Mao was seen as an almost god-like figure.

China Admits Mistakes

Chinese policy began to change after the death of Chairman Mao in 1976. A new leader, Deng Xiaoping, emerged. He was willing to admit mistakes in past policy toward Tibet. People were released after spending years in prison. Nobles received payments for the losses they had suffered.

Return to Tradition

After Chinese policy changed, Tibetans were quick to return to some of their traditional practices. They once again wore traditional clothes, and they began repairing some of the destroyed monasteries.

HOT SPOT BRIEFING

VISITORS FROM EXILE
In 1979 and 1980, official groups from the exiled Tibetan government in Dharamsala, India, were allowed to visit Tibet. Many Tibetans greeted them enthusiastically. The Chinese saw this as a sign that support for an independent Tibet was still strong.

Riders celebrate at the colorful festival of the legendary King Gesar. After Mao's death, some traditional Tibetan customs and practices, previously forbidden, began to be allowed.

MODERNIZATION

During the 1980s, China introduced reforms that aimed to boost its economy and encourage **modernization**. Tibet and the other less developed western regions of China were among the targets.

New policies in Tibet

The reforms meant that the Chinese government introduced new policies in Tibet. The idea was that if Tibetans became wealthier, they would realize the advantages of being part of China. The communes were abolished and farmers went back to working for themselves, selling their produce at market.

HOT SPOT BRIEFING

TIBETAN ECONOMY
The reforms of the 1980s helped Tibetans to become better off, but Tibet is still a poor region. It is the lowest rated of the 31 provinces of China on the UN Human Development Index.

Tibetans harvest barley in fields outside of Lhasa. China has invested heavily in Tibet, but most Tibetans still live by growing basic foodstuffs.

Updating Tibet

Tibet needed up-to-date facilities, such as roads and power stations. The government spent billions of yuan (Chinese money) on such projects from the 1980s onward.

Immigration

Workers from other parts of China went to live in Tibet to work on the modernization projects. This was partly because few Tibetans had the necessary training or skills to do such work. However, some Tibetans believed that the newcomers were part of a plan to increase the number of Chinese people in Tibet.

HOT SPOT BRIEFING

TOURISM
China realized that tourism could become a valuable source of income for Tibet, so it began to welcome increasing numbers of foreign visitors. In 2007, more than four million Chinese and 150,000 foreign tourists visited Tibet.

In 2005, a decorated train marks the completion of the Qinghai–Tibet railway, linking Tibet with the rest of China. Some Tibetans suspect that the railway will be used to bring growing numbers of Chinese into Tibet.

TIBET TODAY

Tibet is still making headlines. Exiled Tibetans and their supporters regularly hold demonstrations against China. On the other hand, many Chinese are angered by what they see as outside interference in their country's affairs.

China in Control

China keeps a firm grip on Tibet. The Chinese government claims that it is simply maintaining order, but critics accuse it of using brutal force. Throughout China, newspapers and TV are strictly controlled, and foreign journalists' activities are restricted.

HOT SPOT BRIEFING

CONTINUING DEVELOPMENT
China has continued to invest heavily in developing its poor western regions, including Tibet. In 2006, the Qinghai–Tibet railway opened, and in January 2009 the government announced a plan to build Lhasa's first highway.

Chinese domination of Tibet is displayed at a festival in the town of Nakchu. Many PLA soldiers are present, alongside portraits of Chinese leaders past and present.

Tibetan Anger

Many Tibetans remain angry that China refuses to grant Tibet greater control over its affairs. Dates such as the anniversary of the Dalai Lama's escape into exile can spark demonstrations. In March 2008, peaceful protests turned into riots. The police restored order by force.

Failed Talks

Talks between China and the Dalai Lama have failed. The Dalai Lama has accepted that Tibet is a part of China, but demands greater autonomy and the protection of traditional culture. China remains unwilling to give up any of its power over Tibet.

HOT SPOT BRIEFING

ANNIVERSARY OF EXILE
March 2009 was the fiftieth anniversary of the Lhasa uprising. The Dalai Lama thanked India for half a century of hospitality. In July 2009, a photographic exhibition opened in Taipei, Taiwan, to celebrate fifty years of campaigning by the Tibetan exile community.

Following the government crackdown on the March Lhasa riots, world interest focused on Tibet in the run-up to the 2008 Beijing Olympics. Pro-Tibetan groups held numerous protests. Scenes like this one, from an anti-Chinese demonstration in Sydney, Australia, were typical.

PLEASE HELP TIBET

FACTFINDER: Tibet

Full name Tibet Autonomous Region

Capital Lhasa

Area 471,700 square miles
(1,221,600 square kilometers)

Population 2,840,000 (2007 estimate)

Rate of population change +1.1% per year

Life expectancy 67 years

Ethnic groups Tibetan 95.3%

                Han Chinese and others 4.7%

Literacy Men 66.5%

         Women 43%

Gross Domestic Product* per person US$1,572

Percentage of labor force in agriculture 16%

Percentage of labor force in industry 39%

Percentage of labor force in services 55%

DISPUTED FACTS

Most facts about Tibet are contested. For example, Tibetan exiles claim that the Chinese are overrunning Tibet, and now make up more than half of the population. The Chinese government, however, counts the Chinese in Tibet at less than 5 percent of the TAR's population.

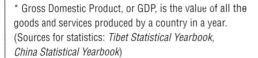

* Gross Domestic Product, or GDP, is the value of all the goods and services produced by a country in a year.
(Sources for statistics: *Tibet Statistical Yearbook,*
China Statistical Yearbook)

FOCUS QUESTIONS

These questions might help you to think about some of the issues raised in *Tibet.*

Leadership and Government

What kind of different styles of government have Tibetans experienced since 1900?

Economy

In what ways did Tibet's economy change after China took over the government? Are China's attempts to modernize Tibet justified?

Politics

Why is Tibet of such interest to people from other parts of the world?
What efforts have other governments made to affect the situation in Tibet?

Citizenship

Do you think the majority of people in Tibet, and in China, support Chinese control?
Have the rights of Tibetans improved or got worse since the Chinese takeover?

The flag of Tibet

GLOSSARY

Buddhist follower of Buddhism, a religion based on the teachings of Buddha

Central Intelligence Agency (CIA) U.S. agency that gathers information on other countries and performs secret missions

civil war war between different groups within their own country

culture things that make a society or people distinctive, such as their language, clothes, food, music, songs, and stories

empire large group of countries ruled by a single country

executed killed as a punishment

exile forced absence from one's own country

guerrilla hit-and-run fighter, often one who aims to overthrow a government

heritage elements of culture that are passed from one generation to another, such as historical buildings or traditions

human rights basic rights such as freedom of speech

minority smaller group within a larger group or population

modernization bringing up to date by using the latest ideas and technology

monarchy system of government headed by a king or queen

monk man who devotes himself to religion, withdrawing from everyday life

nationalist wanting power or independence for one's own country

nomads herders who move from place to place to find food for their herd animals

overlord someone recognized as a superior or protector

parliament group of members or representatives of a political nation

propaganda persuasive information or publicity

province administrative region of a country

reforms social or political changes

republic political system without a royal head of state

resolution formal statement or decision agreed at a meeting

sect section of a larger religious group

treaty formal agreement

United Nations organization set up after World War II that aims to help countries end disputes without fighting

Western characteristic of North America and Western Europe, and their systems of electing governments

INDEX